How to Potty Train
Your Puppy

by Thomas A. Beitz

How To Potty Train Your Puppy

Author: Thomas A. Beitz, Canine Behavior Specialist

ISBN: 978-1-935018-84-1

Interior Design: Leo Ward
Cover Design: Brandon Johnson and Tom Beitz

Published by:
Five Stones Publishing
a division of:
The International Localization Network
ILNcenter.com
info@ilncenter.com

Contents

Forward

I can think of few pleasures in this world that exceed the love, belonging and companionship of having a canine by one's side. Dogs have been in partnership with humans for some 10 to 15 thousand years and there are some social scientists that have opined human civilization would not have been possible without Canis Familiaris. Even to the casual observer of dog breeds, the importance of this relationship becomes evident based on how many different types, sizes, shapes, temperaments and other characteristics of man's best friend there are.

As a veterinarian, there are times this can present quite the medical challenge, and perhaps no greater challenge awaits the experienced and non-experienced dog connoisseur than housebreaking. To this day many outdated and even harmful practices exist for the purposes of housebreaking our pets. Although infrequent, I still hear of frustrated owners striking or even "rubbing their noses in it" to correct wayward bathroom habits. Sometimes pets are surrendered to local shelters, or rescue organizations because owners have reached their breaking point.

For years we lacked an effective, gentle, common sense approach to housebreaking, and related training, from the moment we shared a domicile. "How to Potty Train Your Puppy", by Thomas A. Beitz, provides this in an easy to read, step by step format that will be effective in even the most difficult situations. No longer does potty training your dog have to be an enigma or something to loathe. I am confident you will find his book enlightening and a pleasant read. It should be required reading for anyone who has a dog in need of such training.

James T. Albert DVM

City Creatures Animal Hospital, Buffalo, NY

www.CityCreaturesBuffalo.org

Former Veterinarian for the Buffalo Zoo

Introduction

Why You Need This Book Now

Bringing a new puppy or dog into the home can be just as exciting as bringing a new baby home from the hospital. Although there may be some similarities between your baby and a puppy, there are some distinct differences. Changing your baby's diapers comes with the territory, but changing your wall-to-wall carpeting because your new canine companion just destroyed it doesn't have to be the consequence of bringing a new dog into your home.

Whether you have an eight-week old puppy, an eight-year old dog from the shelter, a tiny three pound Maltese, or a 180 pound giant Mastiff, you can teach your dog proper house manners using my quick, easy-to-follow, common sense housebreaking system. A well-trained dog is a loving family member and companion, but the untrained, unruly dog can be a destructive vexation.

If your goal is to be able to have your dog learn that his bathroom is outside and having freedom inside your home is the reward for good behavior, then this book is the solution to your housebreaking and chewing problems.

Money Back Guaranty

I am so confident that my housebreaking book "How to Potty Train Your Puppy" will work for you I am offering a 100 percent money-back guaranty. If your dog isn't housebroken after following these easy step-by-step instructions for 30 days, I will refund the full price of this book, no questions asked. Although you will see results within a few days, it takes a little time to build new habits.

If you purchased this book through a source other than me, then I probably do not have your contact information. If you'd like to receive my FREE monthly e-newsletter with "Tom's Training Tips" sign up on my website, as well as register for your guaranty. I can be found on the Web at www.smartdogsolutions. com or email me at tom@smartdogsolutions.com.

Training a dog is not rocket science, but there is some science involved. Once you know the scientific secrets the pros have been using for decades, you'll think to yourself, "that's just common sense." A crate is a training tool. Any training device must be used properly in order to be successful. Success is closer than you think even if you have been using a crate with limited success.

There is nothing worse than getting up in the morning before work and discovering that your dog has soiled his crate or left you a mess before you even start your day. Unless, of course, you find the same when you get home from work at the end of a long day. Or, you just stood outside in the rain with your dog for 30 minutes and he didn't go to the bathroom. When you brought him back inside he emptied his bladder and his bowels on the living room rug within 60 seconds of having him out.

According to the Humane Society, over 70% of puppies and dogs are surrendered to shelters as a result of an unresolved behavior or obedience problem. Housebreaking is at the top of the list. This book was written to train the eight-week-old puppy up to the older dog just adopted from your local shelter. I have written this book with smaller breed dogs in mind because it is often thought that they are harder to housebreak. The truth be known, all dogs train the same way, but by taking into consideration some breed-specific characteristics you'll be successful with the most stubborn dog. So why do many people have incredible difficulty housebreaking their furry friend and bundle of love? That is a good question, and I am glad you asked.

Eight Reasons Why People Struggle With Housebreaking

There are eight reasons why people fail to teach their puppy or dog good housebreaking skills. In this owner's manual you will learn how to avoid these common mistakes and get your dog housebroken faster than you could have ever imagined. The same training principles that apply to housebreaking apply to the dog that chews inappropriate personal property, which is another problem addressed in Chapter Seven of this book.

    1. Dog owners give their dog far too much freedom before the dog understands that its bathroom is outside. Pet owners are giving their dog access to the whole house when he can't even find the front door. You're letting

your dog roam around when you wouldn't let a baby. Learn how to supervise your puppy.

2. Many people don't understand the benefits of using a crate or a cage for the purpose of housebreaking a dog. Giving a dog too large an area unsupervised will actually contribute to the dog having accidents in the house. Learn how to utilize the crate effectively.

3. People let their puppy or dog graze or have access to unlimited food and water all day long. Grazing will hinder a dog's ability to develop regular elimination habits. Learn how to establish a good feeding schedule.

4. People fail to recognize the signs that their dog needs to eliminate. Most dogs offer all sorts of body language or rituals before they eliminate. Learn the body language signals.

5. The dog doesn't let you know he has to go to the bathroom. Some dogs won't bark or whimper to let you know they need to go outside. Learn how to teach your dog how to let you know he needs to go out.

6. If you have been using a crate and find your dog is eliminating in the crate, your crate may be too large for the dog. Dogs will generally not eliminate where they sleep unless they have enough room to eliminate and move away from their mess. If a dog is sick or left for too long a period of time he may eliminate also. If a blanket or towel is left in the crate the dog may eliminate on it and push it out of the way so he doesn't have to

lie on it. Learn how to solve the problem of the dog that eliminates in his crate.

7. Paper training is actually teaching your dog to eliminate inside your house. Is that really what you want? Learn why even the small dog can eliminate outside without the need for teaching him to eliminate on paper.

8. You take your dog outside to find a place to go to the bathroom and wait for 30 minutes, and your dog does nothing. You bring the dog back inside, and within 60 seconds your dog has an accident on your new carpet. You begin thinking to yourself that your dog has a serious learning disability. Learn the real secret of housebreaking: confinement.

All of these problems are really not dog problems but operator problems. This book will help you make the necessary changes in your behavior to get your pet started out on the right paw. Guaranteed or your money back!

I know that saying it is an owner/operator problem is not the most diplomatic statement to make. However, this book is not written on the subject of diplomacy; it is written with a money-back guaranty to get your dog housebroken. Think of this book as an operator's manual for housebreaking without the impoverishing mentality of political correctness. The sooner I get to the point, the sooner you will have your canine companion housebroken.

When you understand the common mistakes people make housebreaking their dog, you'll be able to avoid them. Knowing exactly what simple steps you need to follow will empower you to housebreak your puppy or dog faster than you could have ever imagined, seeing results in just a few days.

After you have had a chance to read this dog training book and begun to implement this training strategy and after you have had some success, I hope you'll contact me to let me know about it. I have worked with thousands of dog owners over the years, and I know the frustrations, irritations and disappointments they have experienced. I have also seen dog owners brought to joyful tears at seeing their once out-of-control dog now obedient and well-behaved.

Implementing this information will not only benefit you and your dog, it will benefit the other people in your life. Write to me soon so I can hear about your success. I love to hear good news. Questions? Email me as I am always adding new Q and A material on my website for the benefit of everyone.

Your Canine Consultant,

Thomas A. Beitz

Tom@SmartDogSolutions.com

www.SmartDogSolutions.com

Chapter 1

Why Use the Crate?

Over the years I have been amazed at how many people perceive the use of a crate for training a dog as cruel. If someone were to put their child into a crate, that might be cruel. However, I am convinced that there are an increasing number of children that could benefit from some crate time. I guess we call it "time out" now. There was a time when mothers used playpens to contain their children when they weren't able to monitor their behavior. I hope I haven't offended you by comparing your dog to your child. But I will promise you this, if you follow my instructions I will have your dog housebroken far sooner than your child is potty trained.

Dogs Have a Den Instinct

The reason crates or cages (I use these terms interchangeably) are such an effective training tool is that dogs have what is known as a "den instinct." This instinct can be observed with wild dogs. Dogs will dig a hole in a location that is inconspicuous and crawl into it to sleep or whelp a litter of puppies. The den is a confining place for a dog and, as a result, dogs will not eliminate where they sleep. This hole or den also provides the dog with an increased sense of safety and security from other predators. This is why you may see your dog crawl under a coffee table or fall asleep behind the couch. He is instinctively looking for a place where he can feel safe while he sleeps. Understanding this instinct is a valuable piece of information if used for the purpose of training.

What Kind of Crate is Best?

Basically, there are two types of crates sold. There are metal crates, and there are plastic crates. Metal crates are more open, and the plastic crates appear to be more confining and enclosed. So, which is best? Good question. I think some people prefer the metal crate because the dog will be able to see outside the crate and perhaps feel a little freer. If we apply what we learned about a dog's den instinct, we would be inclined to favor the plastic crate. Personally, I am partial to the plastic crates for the reason I just mentioned. Dogs prefer a dark, safe, secure place to rest. In addition to being more confining (which the dog will prefer), it is also helpful when transporting a dog in the car. When the dog is in the crate and the wind is blowing through the car window, the dog's fur is less likely to blow around the car. If the dog should happen to have an accident, it will be contained in the plastic crate and easier in most cases to clean up. Transporting a dog in a crate is a much safer way to travel. Some states are beginning to legislate automobile restraint requirements for dogs.

If you already have a metal crate, you should use it. You can always cover it with a blanket when leaving the house for work or going to bed at night. Some dogs might attempt to pull the blanket into the metal crate, but you may find that the metal crate works fine without covering it.

Size Matters

How big should the crate be? Another great ques-

tion. Thanks for asking. Ultimately you will want a crate that will be big enough to contain your dog when he is full grown. What does "big enough" actually mean? Your dog should be able to stand up, turn around and lay down comfortably. He does not need a crate the size of a gymnasium in order to be comfortable. Remember, we are trying to simulate a den in the wild.

When you have a small puppy that will become a larger dog when full grown, you will need to begin your young pup in a smaller area which is big enough for him to turn around and lie down. If you buy a large crate because you know your puppy will some day grow into it, you'll find that he eliminates on one end of the crate and hangs out in the clean end. The one advantage of metal crates is that some models are equipped with an adjustable partition. These are convenient because you can make the area the puppy sleeps in much smaller and increase the area of the crate as the pup grows. A dog will generally not eliminate where it sleeps, so the area needs to be small enough so if your puppy or dog does eliminate, he will have to sit or lie in it. Your dog may have one or two accidents when first getting started, but then he'll learn to hold his bladder and bowels until he gets outside to eliminate.

I do prefer the plastic crate, but the metal crate has the advantage of adjustable partitions when training the younger puppies. I have used a box or some other object inside the plastic crate to partition it off. Sometimes you just have to work with what you have and improvise. Your puppy will one day be full grown, and you won't have the need for partitions.

Some people like to put a blanket or a towel in the crate to make it more comfortable for the dog while sleeping. This really isn't a good idea at the beginning of the crate training. The dog will learn that if he has to eliminate, he can go on the blanket or towel and then push it away. The whole idea of crate training is that if the dog eliminates in the crate, he will have to sit in it until you rescue him from his own mess. Dogs naturally won't soil their own den, but during the learning process they need to develop bladder and bowel control. Until your dog has demonstrated control, it would be best to skip any bedding.

Speaking of bedding, I think every puppy thinks it's his job to trash at least one doggie bed in his lifetime, especially when he is inside his crate. The reason a dog will trash his doggie bed is because he is either anxious or bored. Anxiety and boredom are two emotions that elicit destructive behavior in many dogs. It is like a nervous person that chews his fingernails. Until the dog is more mature and confident being left alone, leave the doggie bed in the family room and give your dog a rawhide, a toy or some other chewy when he is in the crate. In chapter seven I explain in more detail what you should do for the dog that chews on everything.

Using the Crate For Training

The two most frequent complaints I get from new puppy owners is that their puppy is not housebroken and that their puppy is very destructive when left unsupervised. These are two of the problems which can easily be resolved with a crate. Exceptions to the rule might include an extremely young puppy that has not developed any bladder control and may need to be let out more frequently, or a dog that is sick with a bladder infection or diarrhea. Certainly if you think your dog is sick you should take him to the vet and have him examined to rule out any medical issues before training begins. Most puppies and dogs are not the exception, and you should be able to get your dog started the first day he enters your home.

The overwhelming majority of puppies and dogs should naturally acclimate themselves to a crate. It is common for a new puppy that has just left his littermates and separated from everything he has ever known to appear to object to being in the crate. The puppy's objection may come in the form of a temper tantrum, barking, whining or any number of other antics. It is not so much that the puppy is objecting to the crate as it is experiencing the distress from being away from his mother and littermates. Anyone who has ever had a baby knows that at some point you need to learn to let the baby cry until it stops.

It is important to keep in mind that dogs learn by association. If the dog begins to have a tantrum and you open the door to the crate, your dog has just learned that if it makes enough noise, you will come and let the dog out of the crate. Then who is training whom? Your dog is training you. Don't let your dog control you to get what he wants. With that being said, you will want to begin to develop an ear for your dog's different vocal communications, just as a mother recognizes her baby cries for different reasons. One cry is for a diaper change, one for a bottle feeding and another for fear. There may be a time when your dog is crying because it really needs to go outside and he doesn't want to soil his crate. At first you may not be able to discern the difference in your dog's vocalization. If that is the case and your dog begins to cry while in the crate, then let the dog out and give the dog a chance to eliminate outside. If after 5 to 10 minutes your dog has not eliminated, then return the dog to the crate and ignore his bellyaching. In the process you will begin to recognize the vocal communication your dog is offering. Of course you can give your dog a hug and a kiss and tell him that putting him in the crate is the best thing you could do for him, and some day he'll appreciate it because he won't become another statistic with a rescue group.

Some people feel guilty leaving their dog in a crate for an extended time, so to ease their guilt they will let their dog have entirely too much freedom for too long a time too soon before the dog is ready. It is similar to a parent who monitors her young child until which time the baby is mature enough to be left alone. Leaving a puppy or dog unattended is dangerous for any number of reasons. Freedom is a privilege your dog will need to earn over time when he demonstrates he can be trusted. Until then, he'll learn to embrace his little canine condo until he matures. Think of using the crate as an act of kindness rather than cruelty.

You are providing a safe place for your dog where he can't get into anything that will hurt him, or damage any valuable property either by eliminating on an expensive Oriental rug or chewing on an antique heirloom. If you are serious about housebreaking your dog and preventing damage to your property, perform an act of kindness and get your dog a crate. Hopefully by now you are convinced that a crate is the solution to the problems you have been having, and we can move on and get started. The best way to read this book is to read it through in its entirety to get the "big picture," and then go back to the individual sections that you feel you may need to focus on. Training is progressive in nature and it takes a little time. Results are not instantaneous, but they are certain with concentrated effort. You can do this!

Using the Crate For Discipline, Not!

Most people have heard that you should not use a crate to punish a dog. I have read this in a number of books and frankly it puzzles me because the statement confuses the meaning of punishment. Punishment as defined by B. F. Skinner (the behaviorist who developed Operant Conditioning Theory) is some unpleasant consequence which results in extinguishing some unwanted behavior. If the consequence (unpleasantness) does not inhibit the behavior, then it does not constitute punishment.

Pavlov's Theory of Associative Learning, brings our attention to the need for precise timing in order for a dog to make any kind of an association (see Appendix A - The Basics of Scientific Learning for more details). Let me give you an example. Let's say you walk into your living room and you catch your puppy chewing on your leather sofa and next to the coffee table you discover a pile of poo. Got the picture? Most people would want to stop the dog chewing and clean up the mess. Common sense would dictate that you put the puppy in the crate so you could assess the damage. But the crate is in the family room on the other side of the house. By the time you snatch up your puppy and walk him to the family room and place him in his crate, perhaps 30 seconds have elapsed. Does the puppy know why he is being put in his crate? No. Will putting the puppy in the crate help the puppy to learn not to poo and chew. No! Too much time has elapsed for the puppy to make the proper association. By virtue of Skinner's definition of punishment, putting your dog in the crate for an inappropriate behavior is not punishment but damage control, which is a perfectly legitimate reason for using a crate regardless of what anyone tells you, especially as it pertains to your mischievous puppy.

The erroneous assumption in connection with the crate and punishment is that if you use the crate too often your puppy won't want to go to his crate and will have a negative association with it. There was a time in our culture when our parents would send kids to their bedroom for having done something inappropriate. I suppose it was a chance to reflect on their behavior or a time out. Later that night when it was time to go to bed, do you know any kid who ever said to his parents, "Because you sent me to my bedroom, I don't want to sleep in my room anymore"? Dogs have a den instinct. They like the sense of safety and security a crate provides, so my advice to you is to use the crate whenever you need it. It is a good idea to put a puppy in the crate for a few hours in the morning as well as the afternoon. It is like putting a baby down for a nap. Puppies sleep quite a bit, and their crate is a good place to do it.

Anytime you have a young puppy or an immature dog that can't be trusted on its own, the crate is a perfect solution. Some mischievous dogs may need to spend more time in the crate than you are comfortable with, especially when you are home and feel the dog needs more freedom. I'll elaborate on this when I get to the chapter on chewing, but if you have a high energy dog and don't use the crate, you'll feel like your life has been taken over by a cute, furry monster.

Chapter Summary

The crate is not a substitute for training, but it does provide a stop gap until such time as your dog can be trusted. How long would you let an 18 month old baby crawl around your house unsupervised? What is the difference if you strap an 18 month old baby in a high chair when preparing a meal or put a puppy in the crate? Most puppies sleep in the crate at night and sleep in the crate while you are at work. The point of this discussion is not that the dog is in the crate as much as what are you teaching the dog when it is out of the crate. What you teach the puppy when it is out of the crate will accelerate his learning and help him to mature so you can trust him out of the crate. But if you are reading this book, he's probably not ready. Not just yet.

Now that I have established the reasons why a crate is the most effective method of housebreaking your dog, I think it's time we get started. In the chapters that follow I will explain different aspects of the training process. If you consider one aspect of the process and neglect the others, you probably won't get the results you are looking for. You need to consider that all of the steps work together and should be employed at the same time.

Chapter 2

Confinement is the Key To Housebreaking

The reason confinement is the key to housebreaking your dog is that a healthy dog will not eliminate where he sleeps. If the area is small enough, when he does eliminate he will be forced to sit in his own mess which is very unpleasant. If you observe your dog eliminating in the crate repeatedly, please take your dog to the vet and rule out any medical problems.

Since we know dogs have a natural instinct to avoid eliminating where they sleep, we are empowered to use this instinct in conjunction with the crate to teach your dog that his bathroom is outside. For the younger puppy seven to eight weeks old, you may be limited to three to four hours of confinement (in the crate) before you will need to give the puppy an opportunity to "do his business" outside. I have read different theories or formulas on how long a puppy should be able to "hold it" before giving him an opportunity to eliminate. Some of these formulas have merit but every dog is different with his own breed-specific characteristics, so these formulas are nearly impossible to implement for every dog. Your dog's feeding schedule will play a bigger role in his learning appropriate eliminating habits, which I'll discuss in detail in the next chapter.

This is where a little common sense and observation on your part comes in. If you are following the feeding schedule I elaborate on in the next chapter, there is no need to run the dog outside every 30 to 60 minutes. In fact, this kind of training is conditioning your dog in a pattern of behavior that will come back to haunt you in six months. Every hour your dog will be running to the door wanting to go outside. You'll not have a clue as to whether the dog needs to eliminate or if this behavior is a conditioned response to something you taught him by taking the dog outside repeatedly.

Whether you have just acquired a new puppy from a breeder or adopted a stray from your local shelter, you are going to want to make housebreaking a priority. You'll need to get into the habit of taking your dog outside after a period of confinement in the crate. Our first and foremost objective is to give the dog an opportunity to eliminate outside. Housebreaking should be your primary goal when getting started with a new dog in your home.

Step-by-Step Guide

Step number one. Upon removing your dog from the crate, attach a leash to the dog's collar, walk him to the same door you want him to use later when he can be trusted on his own, ring the bell (which I will describe in a later chapter), repeat the same familiar phrase such as "do your business", "go potty", or "hurry up" several times and then lead your dog to the same area in the yard while still on the leash. Stand in this area and do not permit the dog to pull you somewhere else in the yard.

Step number two. Take your dog to the same spot in the yard to teach him that this is his bathroom. If you can condition the dog to eliminate in one spot, he will do it on his own when he is trained. The advantage of teaching your dog to eliminate in one designated spot is that you won't be finding land mines all over your yard and cleanup will be much easier. This may seem rigid for some people's taste; but the sooner your dog is housebroken, the sooner you can begin to give him more freedom.

Once the dog has "done his business", then you can engage in other activities such as going for a walk or playtime. This is especially important with a younger puppy. If you have a fenced-in yard and permit your pup to run out the door and begin playing before he has gone to the bathroom, he may actually forget why he is there in the first place. When you bring him back into the house, he'll finally remember that he had to go, and leave you an inappropriate deposit somewhere in the house.

Some people prefer to take their dog on a walk to give the dog the opportunity to eliminate. This may be an option for a trained dog, but I still prefer to have the dog eliminate in the same spot at home. I have never been a big fan of taking my dog on an expedition to find a bathroom. When the dog does eliminate, I'm obligated to pick up the poop in a plastic bag and carry it home to discard it. It's just not my thing.

Step number three. After taking your dog out to eliminate, if he should fail to "do his business," then when you bring the dog back into the house immediately put him back into the crate for 30 to 60 minutes. If you give your dog freedom in the house after you have given him the chance to eliminate outside and he doesn't go, I promise you, he will learn to go inside. This is why confinement is the key to housebreaking any dog. He will not go in his crate. If you make him wait another hour in his crate and then take him out again following the same routine described in step number one, sooner or later he'll learn that nothing in his life happens until he does his business outside. That means no play, no walk, no freedom in the house; nothing happens until he does his business outside. Pee and poop first, then play. The simpler we make it, the faster he'll learn it.

Consistency is the Mother of Learning

Getting everyone in your house to follow these guidelines on a consistent basis will mean the difference between success and failure. Well-meaning family members can undermine your training efforts if they are not on the same page. In fact, this is probably the single greatest problem many families face. Everyone seems to have his own idea on how to train the dog. Maybe one thinks the dog should be able to pull them all over the yard and sniff every bush before it can go. Maybe another thinks that since the dog had 20 minutes of playtime and didn't go when given the opportunity, that he really didn't have to go anyway. As soon as they bring the dog back into the house, the dog has an accident. Let's get everyone on the same page and watch how quickly your dog learns. This doesn't apply to just housebreaking. It applies to walking on a loose leash, jumping up, nipping, chewing, and any other dog training you can think of.

Extreme Case History

I want to tell you a story about a two-year-old Pomeranian I trained about 10 years ago. I got a call from a desperate woman who told me that her two-year-old Pomeranian she had acquired at eight weeks of age, had never gone to the bathroom outside. Not ever. It had been going all over inside her house but never outside. She told me that her husband was demanding the dog be housebroken or else. Desperate circumstances require desperate action. I recommended this crate-training program and the woman followed the instructions exactly as I have laid them out here. Keep in mind that every dog is permitted freedom only after he has done his business outside and not before.

She called me two days after starting the program to tell me that her dog had spent nearly 20 hours a day in the crate and still had not gone to the bathroom. She was giving the dog about an hour at a time outdoors on a tether. When the dog failed to eliminate, she brought it back into the house and put it in the crate. It is important to remember that this dog was young and healthy. It took the dog nearly two and a half days before it had a bowel movement outside for the first time in its life. After a month of working with her dog, he was finally housebroken and she is back on speaking terms with her husband.

This example is an extreme case and is by far an exaggeration of what most people will ever encounter. My purpose in bringing it to your attention is to provide you with an example of an extreme problem that was resolved without punishment, without surrendering the dog and without having the dog euthanized. However, consider the alternatives. If the dog had failed to get trained, it would have been either euthanized or forced to be surrendered to a shelter. Perhaps someone would adopt this cute little bundle of joy only to later find he has a serious housebreaking problem. Unresolved behavior problems such as this can lead to abuse. It is not uncommon for angry or frustrated dog owners to strike out at a dog that doesn't seem to be learning because he is confused. This is especially true of the smaller breeds.

Housebreaking the Small Dog

Many people consider housebreaking a smaller dog more difficult than a larger breed dog. This is partially true, but mostly false. Smaller puppies and dogs seem to be more fragile and sensitive to changes in weather conditions and that contributes to training challenges. If the ground is wet or has snow on it, the smaller dog is less likely to want to be outside in the first place. Like people, some dogs don't want to be standing in a snowstorm or a rain shower waiting to do their business. As a result, too many people look at their little dog shivering or high stepping around the yard looking for a dry spot so he doesn't get his paws wet, give up and bring the dog back into the house before he has eliminated. Generally, the dog will just find a comfortable spot on the dining room carpet where it's nice and dry!

I'll agree the smaller breeds are more particular about where they eliminate. But I will tell you that you don't need to conjure up some special housebreaking formula for the smaller dog. In fact, the people who have the most difficulty housebreaking their dog are the people who invent exceptions, change the rules and are inconsistent with their dogs. When anyone skips one of the steps, permitting inconsistencies into the system, it undermines the training. As unique as your dog is, he will learn all he needs to know about housebreaking the same way larger breed dogs do. The only difference is that you'll need to be more vigilant.

Setting Up Your Small Dog For Success

All of the procedures discussed up to this point remain the same for your small dog. If you begin to think that your small dog is too small or too young to be able to learn how to eliminate outside you will undermine his training. If you take your dog out to eliminate and he fails to do his business, bring him back into the house and put him back in the crate for 30 minutes and then repeat the exercise. He doesn't get any freedom until he eliminates outside.

There are a couple of things you could do to make the trip to the designated area a little more pleasant for your small dog. First, if you have snow on the ground, be sure to shovel a path to the designated area so it is easier for your dog to get there. Secondly, you could put a jacket on your dog so he is not too cold. If it is pouring rain, wait until it subsides, or take your dog out with an umbrella if necessary.

One little trick the smaller dogs will play is that if there is a blanket, doggie bed or towel in the crate, they will eliminate on it and push it out of the way. Take everything out of the crate and make sure the area your dog has is small enough so that if he does go in the crate it will be more unpleasant sitting in his own mess than it is going outside.

Another trick the smaller dogs will pull is to resist going outside at all. You begin tugging on the leash, and the dog sits down and refuses to follow you outside. There are a couple ways of overcoming this resistance. First, assuming your dog is motivated by treats, you could begin pulling your dog up to your side and immediately reward him with a small treat. Then go about six feet away and pull him up to your side and reward him again. The purpose of the treat is to communicate to your dog that when he moves with you, he gets rewarded. If he is motivated by treats, he'll begin to follow you out the door and over to his potty area.

If he is more motivated by avoiding the bad weather conditions and not interested in the treats, which is more likely the case with a smaller dog, you'll need a plan B. Plan B is to simply pick up your dog in the house, clip on the leash, ring the bell, carry the dog to the potty area, set your dog down and follow the same consistent procedure. After 15 minutes, if the dog has not eliminated, bring the dog back inside and put him in his crate and wait about 30 minutes before trying the procedure again.

If you go outside with the intention of your dog eliminating and your dog does not go, bring your dog inside and put him back in his crate. Freedom in the house should be a result of having eliminated outside. No outside elimination, no freedom! It is as simple as that. On occasion accidents will happen. If you analyze the reason for most accidents at this point in the training process, you'll have to admit they are operator (owner) errors and not the dog's fault. If your dog has an accident, clean it up and move on. Unless you can catch the dog in the act, there is no sense disciplining your dog. Disciplining the dog after the fact might make you feel better, but it won't teach the dog anything other than perhaps you're not fair.

Triggers

There are generally three different triggers that will bring about the need for a dog to eliminate. First, after the dog has been sleeping. Second, after the dog has been running and playing and third, after the dog has eaten. If your dog has engaged in any of these activities, take him outside and give him a chance to eliminate. If he doesn't, put him in his crate for 30 to 60 minutes and try the exercise again.

Chapter Summary

After taking the dog into the yard to do his business, if he doesn't go, bring him back into the house and put him in his crate for at least 30 minutes. At the end of 30 minutes, repeat the exercise described in rule number one. At some point your dog will eliminate, then you can give the dog some freedom and have a little fun. The only time a dog should be permitted to have supervised freedom in the house during the initial training period is after he has done his business outside. If you have even the slightest suspicion that he hasn't gone or may need to go, he should be back in his crate. I can't emphasize this enough. The dog is only given freedom in the house after he has done his business outside. When the dog is given freedom, he should be supervised. After the dog has had an hour or two of playtime, put the dog back into the crate for an hour or so and then repeat the exercise.

Now that we have talked about the value of using a crate and how confinement is the key to housebreaking, we need to consider the dog's eating habits. Establishing a regular feeding routine for your dog will contribute significantly to getting your dog housebroken.

Chapter 3

Feeding Schedule Simplified

Establishing a regular feeding schedule for your dog will help in cultivating a regular elimination schedule. Although this training approach seems logical enough to most people, it is surprising how many people leave food and water down for their dog to graze on all day. Permitting a dog to graze on his food and water will actually contribute to the housebreaking problem, especially when it comes to urinating.

When a dog is permitted to lap up water every hour or so, he will have the need to eliminate every hour as well. The fastest and easiest way to develop regular elimination habits is to put him on a strict feeding regimen. I recommend if you have a job and you are not at home for lunch, you should feed your puppy or dog twice per day. If you are retired or at home most of the day and you are able to provide the puppy with a third meal during the middle of the day, you may do so. Never leave food or water in the crate for the dog; doing so could lead to your dog having accidents inside his crate.

The routine is easy to follow. You put the food and water down for 15 to 20 minutes. Allow the dog to eat and drink during the allotted time, then pick up all food and water until the next scheduled feeding. The closer you can keep the dog on schedule, the more regular he will be in his elimination.

Some people seem to think a dog needs to have free access to unlimited water throughout the day. Frankly, unless it is 90 degrees outside and the dog is running around playing, he shouldn't need water more than three times a day. If it is a hot day and your dog is engaged in running about, then by all means, provide the dog with more water. In doing so, you should expect the dog to eliminate more frequently.

If you should happen to have another dog or cats that you leave food and water down for, you will need to pick it up so your dog in training doesn't cheat on his new routine. Once your dog is trained and can be trusted, then you could leave food and water for the other pets in the house. If you have a dog with medical problems that requires more water, then you will need to either provide an area in your home where that dog can get to it or a way the others can't.

As you begin this regimen, you may observe your dog not eating as much during the first day or two. The reason for this is that he has become accustomed to grazing and takes his food for granted. Generally speaking, within two to three days your dog will realize that if he doesn't eat and drink when the food and water are put down, he doesn't get it, and soon he'll begin to chow down like he never has before. The result of this eating routine will prove to be a valuable tool in housebreaking your dog. Your dog will begin to eliminate on such a regular schedule that you will be able to predict it.

The Blessing of Habit - One Simple Rule

The training process is much easier when you have a good understanding of when your dog needs to go out. Your dog will develop a schedule for eliminating as a result of putting him on a regular feeding schedule. As your puppy begins to mature around 12 months of age, you should notice that he may tend to gravitate to either the morning meal or the evening meal. This is generally a sign that your dog is putting himself on a once-a-day feeding. Just combine the two meals and give your dog the entire quantity of food at whatever time he prefers, morning or evening. By keeping your dog on a strict feeding schedule, he will develop a regular habit of eliminating at the same time each day. Permitting your dog to graze will nearly always contribute to housebreaking issues. Don't let your dog graze.

Changing Dog Food

Both puppies and dogs have sensitive digestive systems. If you change your dog's food and you don't make a gradual switch over a period of seven to ten days, you will create your own elimination problem. Changing your dog's food too quickly could result in diarrhea or extremely soft stool. You'll need to give your dog additional opportunities to eliminate when changing foods because he will need to eliminate more frequently.

Some dogs have a cast iron belly and can tolerate eating virtually anything and not get sick, while most other dogs need time to adjust to a change in their diet. If you are changing your dog's food from a puppy formula to an adult formula, do it gradually. The first couple of days mix about 90 percent of the puppy food with 10 percent of the adult food. Observe the dog's stool. If it appears firm, then you can gradually increase the amount of the adult food and decrease the puppy food. If you observe your dog's stool on the soft side, slow the transition from one food to another. You should take about a week to make a complete transition from one formula to another without any problems.

Chapter Summary

For most people you will be feeding your dog twice per day at the same time each day. If you are one of those people who is able to feed your dog at midday the routine remains the same. Put the food and water down for 15 to 20 minutes at a time. Permit your dog to eat and drink during that brief time period. You may want to set a timer to remind you when it is time to pick up the food and water.

Once you have removed the food and water, you do not give the dog anything until the dog's next scheduled feeding. Determine a schedule that works for your lifestyle and stick to it.

Never leave food or water in the dog's crate. This will only lead to other housebreaking problems.

When changing your dog's diet, do it gradually so your dog's digestive system can adjust to the new food.

Chapter 4

Recognizing Your Dog's Body Language

There is one concept that has been repeated throughout this book like a familiar refrain in a song: observation. If you are watching your dog closely when he is out of his crate you should observe all sorts of interesting movements, behaviors and gestures. Each dog is unique with his own personality. With that being said, there are some characteristics of body language that all dogs exhibit in one form or another.

Dogs and people have many things in common as well as some distinct differences. Most of the differences I am referring to are related to specific instincts dogs have that we humans don't. Dogs communicate with their bodies far more often than we realize.

Although this book is not an exhaustive study of a dog's body language, I think it would be helpful to draw your attention to a few body language characteristics connected to a dog's elimination. Being able to recognize just a few body movements will help you in the housebreaking of your dog.

Supervision and observation aren't necessarily the same thing. But since you are going to be doing a lot of supervision over the next few weeks, I'd like to equip you with a few observation tips that will make your housebreaking task a little easier and faster. Supervision is oversight while observation is careful attention to detail for the purpose of arriving at a judgment. Dogs can be almost ritualistic about many of their behaviors and eliminating is one of them. Typically, if you observe your dog over a period of a week or so you will begin to recognize that he engages in certain idiosyncratic behaviors before he eliminates.

Two of the most obvious as well as universal actions are sniffing and circling. Let me give you an example. You may be watching your puppy playing with a toy or chewing on a bone and then suddenly stand up abruptly and begin sniffing the floor profusely. Another sign your dog may need to eliminate is that he may begin circling as he is sniffing. There are scientific reasons why dogs do these things, but frankly you should observe these signs as a precursor to your dog eliminating. If you are playing with your puppy on the carpet in the living room and you observe these rather obvious signs, you want to stop what you are doing and get your puppy out the door immediately. In doing so, your dog will begin to associate these signs with going outside. In time your dog will go to the door before he begins his little ritual.

Sniffing and circling are a couple of the more obvious signs you can look for. However, there are any number of other signs you should recognize as well. Some dogs will seemingly become a little frustrated or agitated and begin barking while others may sneak off in a corner so as not to be seen. My purpose in bringing the concept of your dog's body language to your attention is to help you be more proactive and avoid many of the accidents the unobservant miss. In addition to the body language that relates to elimination, you will begin to develop your own observation skills as they relate to other behaviors your dog might engage in, from interacting with people and other dogs to how he responds to the vet or groomer.

By recognizing these body language signs, you can help shape appropriate responses from your dog in any number of situations. Whether you have just brought home a new puppy or adopted a dog from a local shelter, you'll need to supervise the dog, so you might as well learn to observe him too. Your observations will help you to understand your dog and why he does the things he does.

Accidents do happen. Poop happens too. There may be a few disappointments during the training process when you miss your dog's signs and he leaves you a mess. It is not the end of the world. We certainly want to minimize the number of accidents to as few as possible, but it needs to be understood that it's all a part of learning. In most cases, if the dog doesn't go to the door, he may be offering other signs. Watch for them. Discipline and correction can go a long way if administered properly. Discipline can also be counterproductive if done improperly.

One of the oldest discipline myths connected with housebreaking a dog for having an accident is to rub the dog's nose in his own mess. "Yep, that should do it. He'll never have another accident as long as he lives." The only problem with this method of discipline is that it does not work. It does not teach the dog anything. It may make you feel better for a moment, but it doesn't communicate anything to the dog other than that he doesn't want to be around you in the presence of his bodily fluids. So please, don't use the antiquated, misguided technique.

Marking vs Housebreaking

Marking may be described as a way of a dog establishing his territory by leaving a urine sample where other dogs can smell where he's been. Although marking inside the house is an annoying problem, it is not the same problem as housebreaking. A dog that is marking in a house is trying to establish his territorial mark so other animals such as other dogs or cats know who is on the top of the pecking order. Male dogs tend to mark much more than female dogs, but females can mark also. Some females will even lift their leg like a male to leave their mark. The body language associated with marking is going to be a little different from the normal housebreaking language.

The difference between a housebreaking problem and a marking problem is actually pretty easy to distinguish. The dog that marks will eliminate repeatedly using small amounts of urine to mark different spots. A housebreaking problem is when a dog empties his bladder or bowels in one spot not because he is marking the spot, but because he doesn't know his bathroom is outside.

I should mention a medical issue that gives the appearance of a marking problem when it's not. You may observe a dog begin urinating small amounts frequently during the day even when the dog is in his crate. If the dog has not been piddling in his crate prior to this time but you begin to see he is having difficulty holding his bladder through the night, this problem is most likely a urinary tract infection and not a marking behavior. Younger puppies are prone to these types of infections. If you have any medical questions or concerns, contact your vet immediately.

Most house pets that have been spayed or neutered will be far less likely to develop the behavior of marking. Generally speaking, there are three types of dogs that might be inclined to mark. The first type of dog is the intact male which has been used for breeding purposes. The second type of dog which might be inclined to mark his territory is a dog that has been confined to a kennel or shelter for an extended period of time. They normally have a small area they can call their own, so they will mark it as to communicate to other dogs "this is my space." The older the dog and the longer the dog has been confined, the longer it will take to correct the marking problem. The third type of dog is a feral dog that has never had any training at all and has no clue what proper house manners consist of.

The dog that "marks" is going to be more of a training challenge for the average pet owner. Correcting this annoying behavior will require extreme vigilance. In fact, everything you have learned in this book will have to be magnified, or put on steroids, which means you have a high maintenance dog that will need to be micro-managed anytime he is outside of his crate. The moment you observe the dog even thinking about lifting his leg, stomp your foot and immediately take the dog outside and follow the instructions used for housebreaking discussed in the previous chapters. Yes, you do have to be sort of a mind reader with a dog that marks.

If the dog has not been spayed or neutered, you should consider having it done as soon as possible. Neutering is not necessarily a remedy, but it will certainly contribute to fixing the problem over time, no pun intended. I have counseled people who have worked with an eight-year-old marker for six to eight months before they started to see any significant progress. A dog that marks may be a dog that is not housebroken, but the marking problem is more serious than housebreaking. Crating the dog when you are not able to supervise him is imperative.

There are two other piddling problems which are similar to marking but fall into different categories known as *submissive urinating* and *excitement urinating*. These problems are technically not housebreaking problems because they are either an instinctive or an involuntary response to your dogs surroundings. For a detailed explanation please refer to Appendix B in the back of this book.

Chapter Summary

Look for the signs your dog may need to eliminate. They include sniffing, circling, agitation, frustration or barking. When you are spending time with your dog (especially just before he eliminates) try to observe his body language. The signs are there if you have eyes to see them. Just look.

When you recognize the signs, take him to the door and get him outside as fast as possible.

One of the most obvious signs for the dog that "marks" is sniffing with intention.

Be especially vigilant with the marking dog.

Chapter 5
How Dogs Learn

If you were to summarize all of the learning theories associated with dog training you could boil it down to these distinct teaching principles: timing, motivation and consistency, they are the fundamental building blocks of how dogs learn. As you begin to understand how these principles work together, not only will you be able to housebreak your dog but you will be able to teach your dog just about anything you want.

Timing

Housebreaking is probably one of the first hurdles any new puppy owner will have to get past in the training process. The principle of timing is a familiar theme that is woven through every training method known to mankind. In this chapter I will give you a brief overview of the importance of timing, but if you'd like a more detailed explanation, go to Appendix A and read the *The Basics Of Scientific Learning*.

For well over 100 years we have known that dogs are conditioned-response animals, and they learn by association. However, a dog needs to make that association in about one and a half seconds or less. If we are going to reward a dog or correct a dog for any behavior, it needs to be done almost immediately if the dog is going to make the proper association. Let me give you an example. Let's say you step out of the room for several minutes and when you return you discover your puppy had an accident. You don't know if it happened 20 seconds ago or two minutes ago. What should you do? Nothing. Clean up the mess and move on. In all likelihood it is really your fault and not your puppy's. If you had been following the instructions you have been given up to this point, you would never have left the puppy unattended, or he would have been in his crate until you were able to let him outside.

More importantly as it relates to timing, because you were not present to witness the accident and catch your dog in the act, any discipline would be completely ineffective.

It wouldn't be effective because you need to administer the correction immediately in order for the dog to make the proper association. The association your dog needs to make is that when he has an accident in the house and gets caught in the act, it results in an unpleasant consequence. He won't want the consequence, therefore he will not eliminate in the house. If you can't catch the dog in the act, then you can't discipline the dog effectively.

Motivation

Motivation only comes in two forms, positive motivation and negative. Positive motivation, simply put, is some kind of a reward that turns your dog on. Although treats are commonly used by many trainers, petting and praise, love and affection, toys and other things can be just as effective. The truth is that not all dogs are motivated by treats. Some distractions, such as another dog or a visitor, are more motivating than a treat. So finding what turns your dog on is important. A reward represents the positive side of the equation while discipline represents the negative side of the equation.

Negative motivation (discipline) comes in the form of an unpleasant consequence as a result of an unwanted behavior. The term discipline isn't used much these days, but in the end analysis, punishment, correction and discipline are all words that essentially mean the same thing. Discipline is probably one of the most misunderstood concepts in our society today extending far beyond the boundaries of dog training. It is just one of the topics I discuss in my extensive FREE Report, *What Dog Trainers Don't Tell You.* Get your FREE copy NOW! For the purposes of this book I will limit my instruction to the subjects at hand, namely housebreaking and destructive chewing.

Discipline

You may be thinking "What should I do if I catch my dog in the act of eliminating in the house?" "How do I discipline my dog?" We know rubbing the dog's nose in his own mess is not an option, right? You got that. The most effective method which I have been using for nearly 20 years is as follows: The instant you see your dog squatting to eliminate, stomp your foot on the floor and sternly bark the NO!!! command at your dog. Bark it like you are yelling at your spouse or one of your kids. Your dog needs to understand by the stomping of your foot and the inflection in your voice that something is seriously wrong. He will most likely freeze in his tracks. Then, casually walk over to the dog, change your tone from reprimand to neutral, calmly take the dog by the collar and walk him to the door you routinely use to take him out, and follow the guidelines discussed earlier in this book. When you come back into the house, put your dog in the crate while you clean up his mess, and move on with your life. When you are done with cleaning up the mess you can either leave the dog in the crate or take the dog out of the crate and engage him in some meaningful activity, whichever is more convenient for you. The key to effective training and discipline is catching your dog in the act. The discipline was deliberate, decisive, immediate and lasted about two seconds. That is it! You don't need to turn an accident into a drama production.

Take your dog through the exercise of going outside regardless if he finished his business in the house. We want to establish a routine even in the event of an accident. The day will come when your dog will walk over to the door and bark to let you know he needs to go out. When that day comes, which will be sooner than you think, praise your dog, open the door and take him to his designated bathroom in the yard.

Praise and Reward

The teaching principle of timing applies to praise as it does with discipline. The process is quite simple. You can use either a small motivational treat or petting and praise to reward your dog for eliminating outdoors at his designated location. Wait for your dog to complete the task of eliminating and then immediately reward him. Keep in mind that all he has done was go to the bathroom where he was supposed to and hasn't graduated from Harvard. The reward, whether it be a treat or praise, should be given immediately and last for two seconds, no more. Did you notice that the correction we gave your dog for having an accident lasted two seconds? Good, you can see how these teaching principles work together.

If you give your dog a six ounce Milk Bone or you praise him for 30 to 60 seconds you will lose the value of pairing the reward with the behavior. The association takes place in about one and a half seconds. Anything longer washes out the association and increases the learning curve significantly. This applies to discipline as well as rewards. That is why in my explanation of discipline I suggested a "stomp of the foot and a bark of the NO!" Done. That's it. Anything longer will be of no value and will more than likely be counterproductive. As you begin to apply these teaching principles of timing and motivation, you will begin to see how they will apply to everything you teach your dog.

Consistency

The third teaching principle is one that most people are familiar with, but have the most difficulty following; consistency. It is always going to be more of a challenge in a home where there are several people trying to housebreak the dog at the same time. Getting everyone on the same page can sometimes be a challenge especially when one person is doing one thing and another person is doing something else. When this occurs, you'll begin to see your dog having more accidents. Your dog is really just confused. In fact, this problem of inconsistency among family members may be the number one reason why dogs are not housebroken sooner.

It is the reason for many other behavior problems too. You may not be able to get everyone in your family to read this book, so I have included a Quick Guide to Housebreaking in Chapter Eight. It gives you the essentials in a concise format so everyone knows the game plan. If you are the designated trainer in your household, you'll need to oversee other family members to be certain they are following the instructions.

Chapter Summary

Timing, motivation (positive and negative) and consistency all work together to build a sound foundation for your dog.

When you reward or discipline your dog, do it immediately (within one to one and a half seconds)

Be consistent. Get everyone in your household doing and the saying the same thing.

Chapter 6

Teaching Your Dog to Let You Know He Needs to Go Potty

There are some puppies and dogs that won't let you know when they need to go outside to eliminate. While some dogs will bark, whimper, begin circling or become agitated to let you know they need to get outside, others remain silent. Apart from taking the dog out on a regular basis, you'll never really know when he needs to go out.

One of the most popular ways to help your dog communicate with you is to teach your dog to ring a bell when he needs to go out. This is a case of teaching your dog to teach you. When he rings the bell, you go to the door and let him out. This should be an easy one for us to learn because we have already been conditioned to go to the door when someone rings the door bell.

I have talked to some people who think this method is ridiculous only later to discover it is amazingly reliable and easy to teach to any dog. Some dogs will pick this up in a matter of a couple hours. As with anything you teach your dog, you will find that some dogs actually will learn a new behavior the very first time you show it to them.

Let's get started. Hang a bell attached to a string on the doorknob or the threshold of a door where your dog can reach it with his nose or his paw. Use the same door you normally use to take the dog out to eliminate. Every time you take the dog outside,

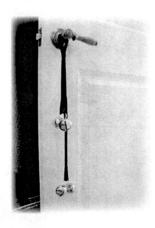

take your dog to the door, ring the bell and repeat your "potty command" we discussed in chapter two. It could be "go potty", "hurry up", "do your business", it really doesn't matter what you say as long as everyone in your family is saying and doing the same thing. Repeat the command several times as you ring the bell, then take the dog outside to the designated area and continue to repeat the command until the dog eliminates. As soon as he does his business, praise him or reward him with a treat. The reward must be given immediately if you want your dog to make the proper association.

Consistency is the mother of learning. As you repeat this simple exercise over time, the day will come when you are not paying attention to your dog and you will hear him ring the bell. As soon as he rings the bell, praise him for taking the initiative and then follow the instructions above. Dogs love it when they can initiate something and recognize you understand what they want. Your dog gets joy when he realizes you understand his request. When a dog goes to an empty water bowl, begins to push it around or bark, and you respond by filling it up, your dog is thinking to himself, "That's what I'm talking about!"

So when your dog does actually ring the bell, you need to get up and take the dog out. Some dogs will learn when they ring the bell you take them out, so they will begin ringing the bell repeatedly because they want to go out every 15 minutes. This doesn't happen often, but it does happen. If you discern that your dog is exploiting his new exercise and driving you crazy, there are a couple of things you can do.

The first time he rings the bell, take him out and follow the usual procedure described earlier in this exercise. If he doesn't eliminate within 15 minutes, bring him back inside and put him in his crate for about 60 minutes. We want to follow the original exercise of teaching him that going outside is first and foremost for the purpose of eliminating. Once he does eliminate, then you can spend some time playing with him in the yard if you wish. Essentially he needs to understand that freedom in the house and play time only happen after he has done his business outside.

Let's examine another possibility. Perhaps he has gone outside and eliminated about 30 minutes ago and then rings the bell to go out again. You know he has already done his business, so you know he doesn't need to go again. You have a couple of options. If you have a fenced-in yard, you could take him out to play with him or let him play in the yard by himself. The other option is to put him back in his crate for 30 to 60 minutes. The reason for putting him back in his crate is to teach him that ringing the bell is for the purpose of going outside to eliminate. This is not punishment. The purpose of putting the dog back into the crate is to maintain strict consistency so he learns to associate the bell with going outside to eliminate.

If you should decide to play with the dog in the yard when he rings the bell, try to initiate the game or playtime yourself rather than letting your dog initiate it. By permitting your dog to initiate various activities he may learn how to control you. Over time he may grow into a dominant, demanding dog. You'll find you won't be able to sit and watch the evening news without being interrupted by your dog insisting on affection or demanding playtime. The first few times a dog initiates something it is cute and humorous. I'm certainly not suggesting that you don't play with your dog, but if you should begin to observe your dog trying to control your life, you may want to begin to be deliberate in your intentions. In other words, lead your dog into some activity that you have initiated. It could be any activity you like, but it should be one that you have initiated, not your dog. These comments are directed toward the dominant, pushy, demanding dog. For more information in dealing with this type of pushy dog, read the article on my website, Boss Dog.

Chapter Summary

Use the same door to take your dog outside to eliminate.

Using the same door, make sure the bell is attached to the wall close enough to the floor where your dog can reach it with a paw or his nose to ring it.

Every time you take your dog outside, ring the bell several times and repeat your "go potty" command.

Take your dog to the same designated spot and repeat the "go potty" command.

Continue to repeat the command until your dog has finished eliminating and then reward your dog with praise ("good boy") or a small treat.

It may take a couple of days or a couple of weeks, but at some point in the training process your dog will go to the door and ring the bell to let you know he needs to go outside.

Chapter 7

BONUS:

Stop Destructive Chewing Forever

There are a number of reasons why puppies and dogs chew. Dog trainers often categorize the different reasons why dogs engage in destructive chewing behaviors. The solutions are limited, yet effective. Before we can consider the solution to the destructive chewing problem, it is important to understand the problem from the dog's perspective. As we begin to understand why dogs chew, we can modify the behavior by creating an environment which directs the dog's focus on productive outlets rather than leaving a dog to his own devices. I am confident as you begin to understand the reasons your dog thinks he is a demolition machine, you will be more committed to engaging your dog in meaningful activities.

Training consists of teaching the dog to respect your personal property, sequestering the puppy when you are not able to supervise, and disciplining the dog when caught in the act of destructive chewing. If you have a "chewer", I'm sure you want the quick fix. You may be thinking, "Just tell me how to keep this dog from destroying my house". We'll get to that, but please read the reasons why dogs chew before you jump ahead to the corrective phase of the training. Prevention is better than damage control.

Nutritional Deficiency

Before we employ any corrective measures to inhibit a destructive chewing behavior, it's always a good idea to rule out any medical issues such as a nutritional deficiency. Many of the problems we have in this country associated with obesity in humans have been connected to nutritional deficiencies. Our bodies are craving one nutrient or another, and we overeat in an attempt to satisfy the hankering. Dogs, however, only get a measured portion of food each day and are not able to snack or gorge like we are. The dog with a nutritional deficiency will resort to chewing on just about anything to satisfy his hankering.

There are myriad reasons why your dog may have a vitamin or mineral deficiency. They include, but are not limited to, a poor quality dog food manufactured with genetically-modified grains used in commercial foods, environmental factors, chemical additives, processed foods or allergies to certain foods and treats.

Apart from having your vet do a complete workup on your dog, you may want to experiment with a higher quality dog food that offers natural ingredients. Due to the chemical-ridden agricultural practices of some commercial farmers, the nutritional value of our food supply has significantly diminished over the past 50 years. Even the best dog foods available may not solve a nutritional deficiency without supplementation. Check with your vet or an animal holistic practitioner for additional information on this important subject. You'd be surprised at how many dogs stop destructive chewing after mineral supplementation was started. A nutrient-deficient dog is not chewing for the same reason as a young puppy teething or a dog that is bored out of his mind. It's important to make the distinction.

Teething

More than likely, if you are working on housebreaking you have a younger puppy and teething is also a problem. When your puppy comes into his juvenile period of development (also referred to as adolescence) he will start to lose his puppy teeth and begin growing his adult teeth. This generally begins around four to five months of age. Your puppy will become very mouthy, which means he will be grabbing and chewing anything he can get his mouth on. When a puppy is cutting his adult teeth, it is similar to a baby teething. He just needs to chew on something to soothe his gums.

Your job is to provide the chewer with a proper outlet. Dogs are as different as people. You should experiment with your dog to discover what type of chew bone or toy he prefers. If you find one he likes, stick with it. He'll be less likely to chew something he shouldn't. Parents will child-proof a room to protect their children from injuring themselves. You'll need to puppy-proof the room to protect your property from being damaged. If you don't leave anything laying around on the floor where your puppy can get at it, you'll save yourself a lot of grief.

I am not a big fan of soft pillow type toys because a puppy can destroy them in a millisecond. There are some breeds, such as retrievers, that have a softer bite and will just carry a soft toy around like a pacifier. However, too many puppies have ingested small toy parts and ended up with bowel obstructions. This is a serious medical issue that could cost you a lot of money if your dog needs surgery. Harder bones and dense plastic chewies are safer for your puppy. I prefer to start a younger puppy out with only one or two chew toys. If your dog is permitted to have 20 different toys to choose from, then it becomes more of a training challenge for a puppy to make a distinction as to what is appropriate and what is not. By limiting your dog to one or two chew toys or bones he'll begin to learn which items are his and which are not. As he gets older you can add more toys to his collection.

For the puppy that is having a lot of difficulty during the teething stage, you may want to try this old but effective home remedy. Take a 3 oz. plastic cup and fill it about halfway with water, then add a Milk Bone and freeze it for a soothing nutritional treat. Remove the cup before giving to your dog. The ice reduces inflammation, soothes the gums and provides the dog with a healthy snack.

There are a number of chewing deterrents that could be used, the most popular of which is known as Bitter Apple. This product is sold in most pet stores. It comes in a spray bottle and can be applied to nearly any surface or object your dog may want to chew. Bitter Apple is a liquid substance that most puppies and dogs find very offensive. You spray the object with Bitter Apple and your dog will avoid it. You may need to spray the area every three or four days until the dog begins to ignore it altogether.

Be sure not to give your dog an old shoe or some other unwanted item to chew on or play with. Your dog won't be able to distinguish between an old, unwanted shoe and a new shoe.

Avoid playing "tug of war" with your puppy. Although it is a fun game, it encourages unwanted chewing and nipping. Playing fetch with your dog is a much more productive game to play because you're providing your dog with needed exercise.

Boredom and Lack of Exercise

Dogs are naturally inquisitive creatures. They thrive on having the opportunity to investigate their surroundings. Restricting a dog over extended periods contributes to all sorts of behavior problems such as destructive chewing. The first part of this book promotes restricting a dog for the purpose of housebreaking. Isn't that a contradiction?

Restricting a puppy or dog for the purpose of housebreaking and providing the dog freedom to explore and engage in other activities are two different things. Once your dog has eliminated, then and only then should you begin to give him freedom to explore. When it comes to dog training, it's necessary to determine what your ultimate objectives are and then prioritize them.

It is interesting that 40 or 50 years ago there were no leash laws. Dogs were permitted to roam the neighborhood and do the things dogs do naturally. Back then, dogs seemed to be healthier, not to mention more rounded and balanced with far fewer behavior problems. Today, we have legislated and regulated our dogs into a behavioral nightmare. Leash laws have seriously limited our dogs' freedom which has unintended consequences. Dogs have instincts that can only be fulfilled when given freedom. The more restrictive we become with our dogs, the more behavioral problems we can expect. Dogs need to be given the opportunity to investigate their surroundings and to have social contact with other dogs and people. Dogs that are given these options will have a higher quality of life with fewer behavior problems. Many people don't consider training their dog off leash when, in fact, it would actually contribute to solving many of the behavior problems they are experiencing.

Obedient dogs have more fun because they enjoy the benefits of freedom. When a dog is genuinely obedience trained, he will come when called even in the presence of extreme distractions. Every time I tell people they should train their dog to come off leash, inevitably I hear, "Not my dog, you could never train my dog to be off-leash reliable." Training a dog to be off-leash reliable is much easier than you might think. Training techniques and technology have significantly improved over the past 15 years. Nearly anyone can train their dog to come off leash even with distractions. Check out my website www.smartdogsolutions.com for the 2013 release of my newest training book, *Off Leash in Three Weeks*.

Anxiety

A dog that is nervous or anxious will chew much like nervous people chew on their fingernails. More often than not, anxiety in a dog is the result of separation which leads to destructive chewing. When younger puppies are not taught to be left alone they can develop separation anxiety. Although many people think their dog's destructive behavior is a spiteful form of revenge for having been left alone it is, in fact, a nervous reaction. A dog with separation anxiety engaging in destructive chewing behavior can no more stop chewing than people who chew their fingernails. Separation anxiety is a completely different subject worthy of further discussion. However, I will comment on it here briefly because the problem is becoming increasingly more widespread.

The most commonly-accepted remedy for separation anxiety is the use of a crate. If you are not able to watch your puppy like a hawk, then the puppy should be in his crate. Younger puppies may object to the crate initially, but generally the dog will learn to love it if you stick with it. One of the reasons why separation anxiety is on the increase is because when a puppy or dog has a temper tantrum in the crate, the owner lets the dog out which reinforces the temper tantrum. In the crate, the dog is not able to injure himself nor is he able to damage any of your property. Certainly, if your dog is being destructive, he is not ready to be left alone in the house unattended or unsupervised. So if you are not able to micromanage your puppy's activities, he should be in the crate.

Chewing for Attention

The more structure and training you provide for your puppy, the better behaved he will be. Unfortunately too many people are reactive rather than proactive when it comes to their puppy. If our goal is to just "stop" the puppy from bad behavior, our job will seem time-consuming, laborious and frustrating. If we engage our puppy with meaningful tasks, training exercises and play, our interaction will be instructive, helping to shape our dog's understanding of the world around him.

Dogs want to be engaged. They are social animals. If your focus has been on damage control, your dog will begin to recognize when he engages in any inappropriate behavior, he can get our attention; he will begin to solicit your attention every chance he has. If he thinks you are ignoring him, he will grab one of your shoes, and you'll engage him by chasing him through the house trying to catch him. This is a game many puppies have perfected and one of their favorites. Your dog is getting you to do what he wants. He's initiated a game and in the grand scheme of things, learning to control you. He is taking the lead and you are the follower. Providing your dog with an obedience exercise on a daily basis will empower you to be the proactive leader you need to be. Obedience training is akin to spending quality time with your kids. Quality time provides structure and direction which naturally results in fewer problems. However, when problems do surface, they need to be dealt with deliberately and decisively.

Disciplining Chewing Problems

The concept of discipline has gone from one extreme to the other over the past 50 years. During the 1950s, harsh corrective measures were advocated which I'm reluctant to even mention in this book for fear they would be considered abusive by today's standards. The suggestions offered by contemporary trainers would hardly constitute discipline at all, but more likely reinforcement. Dog training theory has been based on "consequences" because that is just how nature works. If you could train your dog with love and affection, treats and praise alone, my guess is you wouldn't be reading this book or scouring the Internet looking for help.

Assuming you have followed the recommended guidelines to prevent chewing, here is one approach you can use to discipline your dog when you catch him in the act of destroying your property.

First, never discipline your dog out of anger. It will be counterproductive to your relationship with your dog. Discipline needs to be administered calmly, assertively, deliberately and decisively.

Second, in order for discipline to be effective, it has to come at the moment of the infraction (immediately). If you walk into a room and discover your dog has mistaken your leather sofa for a rawhide chewy, unless you can catch him in the act, disciplining him after the fact will not teach your dog anything.

Third, if you are able to catch your dog in the act of engaging in destructive chewing, then follow these instructions: stomp your foot on the floor and sternly bark "NO!!" at your dog. Startling your dog will help him to associate the stern "NO!" with his chewing. This form of correction works with most dogs, and although it will not necessarily prevent your dog from chewing in an unsupervised situation, he will learn not to chew in your presence. As he learns not to chew in your presence, in time he'll learn not to chew when left alone.

If you have a puppy or dog that is constantly looking for something to get into, then you'll need to have a leash attached to the dog at all times (supervised) until such time as he learns proper house manners. Some dogs that persist at chewing will need a physical correction such as a jerk on the leash along with a stern "NO!". If you find your dog qualifies as being persistent, grab the leash and give it a firm tug (this is called a leash correction) while saying "NO!". The added physical correction may leave a better impression on the more stubborn dog. Generally, one leash correction and stern "NO!" should be adequate to stop the chewing. After the correction, you should redirect the dog's attention to something more productive such as a brief two or three minute obedience exercise or a short walk in the neighborhood. When you complete the obedience exercise, then you could reward your dog with a chew bone or a toy.

By giving your dog a bone or toy immediately after catching him in the act of destructive chewing, you may inadvertently be rewarding him for the very behavior you wish to eliminate. I prefer to redirect the dog with obedience training first by reinforcing good behavior, establishing the owner as the leader and then looking for something positive to reward after a few minutes.

If you have a younger puppy, he shouldn't be left unsupervised. If you have just adopted an older dog from a local shelter, you will need to observe the dog over a period of about a month to be certain he doesn't have any unresolved behavior problems. You cannot assume because you have adopted what appears to be an older, more mature dog that he is well-behaved and doesn't have any issues. This recommendation may seem stringent to some, but until your canine companion has demonstrated he can be trusted, he needs to be supervised at all times. If you are not able to supervise your dog, then he should be in his crate. Some dogs will spend what seems to be a lot of time in the crate, and you may be inclined to feel guilty. These are normal feelings, but until your dog is properly trained, you'll need to be strong and follow through with the training instructions.

Your dog can spend time out of the crate as long as you are able to supervise him. As a culture, we are far too permissive with our pets and this is what is, at least in part, contributing to many of the problems we are experiencing. Training takes time and effort.

As your dog begins to mature and learns to respect your personal property, then you will be able to give your dog more freedom on a gradual basis. Not only do you gradually give your dog freedom, you continue to limit the dog to one or two rooms in the house to see how well he does on his own. Going from crate confinement to complete freedom throughout the house is asking for trouble.

We live in a busy world with more options than any other generation in the history of civilization. It's not unusual for people to work 10 to 12 hour days. If you have a puppy, you'll feel like he is spending most of the day and night in the crate. Yes, he is, but this is only temporary until he matures and can be trusted. Keep your eyes on the goal of having a loving, well-behaved companion you can trust. It takes time for a puppy to mature, so don't expect perfection immediately. As your dog learns his boundaries and becomes comfortable with his surroundings, you can begin to give him more freedom each month as he earns your trust.

I have seen some puppies gain complete freedom throughout the entire house at seven months of age, while there are other dogs that never earn unsupervised freedom in the house. No two dogs are alike. Assuming your dog is on a good diet, getting plenty of exercise along with obedience training, he should grow into a well-balanced mature dog that can be trusted alone. It takes time, so don't expect an overnight sensation.

Chapter Summary

We should have accomplished the following guidelines before we consider disciplining our dog for destructive chewing.

First, you should have your puppy on a quality dog food and have ruled out a possible nutritional deficiency.

Second, you should be offering ample opportunity for your dog to get enough exercise each day that results in getting the dog tired. A tired dog is a happy dog.

Third, you should provide the dog with one or two choice chew toys or bones and teach him that these are acceptable items to chew on.

Fourth, you should have your dog accustomed to going into his crate without objecting during the day when you are unable to manage the dog's activities.

Fifth, you should be engaging your dog in meaningful obedience training exercises and playtime each day, teaching him to respect property and follow your lead.

Sixth, during the teething period of your dog's development, you'll need to be extra vigilant in supervising your puppy.

Finally, when the time comes and discipline is warranted, it should be done immediately. You need to catch the dog in the act in order for the dog to make the proper association. The correction should be decisive and brief. Excessive discipline is abuse. The correction should last no more than two seconds and then redirect the dog away from the situation.

Putting your dog in his crate after catching him engaged in an inappropriate behavior is NOT punishment despite what you may have heard. The reason it is not punishment is because genuine punishment will stop a bad behavior from reoccurring. Putting a dog in his crate will not stop a dog from engaging in bad behavior in the future so it is not punishment. It may constitute a "timeout" but it is not punishment. The crate is the dog's den where he can feel safe and secure; it's a place where he can be contained while you have more important things to tend to.

Chapter 8
The Quick Guide to Housebreaking

In this chapter, I will be summarizing the entire Housebreaking System, providing you with all the essentials you need to get your dog housebroken now. If, in the process, you discover this compressed summary is not adequate, please go back and read the more detailed information. It is not unusual for someone to come very close to housebreaking his dog only to find out the dog isn't completely trained. It may be a matter of one small aspect of the program which needs to be fine-tuned.

You will need a crate. It needs to be small enough so if your dog eliminates while in the crate he will have to sit in his own mess, yet large enough to accommodate your dog as he grows. Some crates provide a movable partition so you can make the crate as small or as large as needed. As you begin the training, do NOT put any bedding or towels in the crate. Putting a blanket or towel in the crate provides the dog a place to eliminate and he will push it out of the way so he doesn't have to sit in his own mess. If the dog has an accident in the crate, we want to make it unpleasant for him so he chooses not to go in the crate. A healthy dog will not eliminate where it sleeps.

Your dog needs to be on a strict feeding schedule. Put the food and water down twice per day (morning and evening) for 15 minutes at a time. Give your dog 15 minutes to eat his meal and drink the water provided. After 15 minutes, pick up both the food and water and don't give the dog anything to eat or drink until his next scheduled feeding. Dogs that are accustomed to grazing may not eat for a couple of days. However, he will figure out if he doesn't eat in the allotted time, he doesn't get fed. He'll begin to chow down when given the opportunity. Establishing a regular feeding schedule will help to develop a regular elimination routine for your dog. If you are training your dog during the hot summer months, you will need to be certain your dog is getting enough water to prevent dehydration.

Take your dog outside to the same spot each time using the same door to get into the yard. Your only purpose for taking your dog outside to the designated area is to establish the habit of going to the bathroom outside. After the dog eliminates, you can take him for a walk, play with him in the yard or bring him back into the house. If you go outside for the purpose of eliminating and your dog does NOT do his business and you bring him back into the house, he should be put back in his crate for 30 to 60 minutes and then repeat this sequence. Your dog is NOT permitted any freedom in the house until he has done his business outside. This is the cardinal rule associated with housebreaking. No elimination, no freedom. It's really that simple. The key to housebreaking is confinement.

When your dog has eliminated outside and you want to begin giving him freedom in the house, you need to limit that freedom to one or two rooms at a time. As your dog begins to associate outdoors with eliminating and he hasn't had any accidents in three or four weeks, you can gradually give him more freedom in the house. If he should have an accident, then you go back to limiting his freedom. Limiting the area your dog has to roam makes it easier to supervise your dog.

There are three activities that generally trigger the need to eliminate.

One, he has just eaten. He'll need to eliminate within 5 to 30 minutes.

Two, he has just awakened from a nap. Let's say you have fed your dog at 5 pm and he's done his job by 5:30 and you've brought him back into the house to play with him. After about an hour of playtime he crashes and takes a nap. As soon as he wakes from his nap, you should take him back out. Chances are he will need to go again.

Three, he has been running and playing inside or out; he will more than likely need to eliminate soon after. You have the responsibility to observe your dog and learn his body language. By recognizing the signals, you can help your dog learn faster by getting him outside before there is an accident.

If your dog goes to the door and is trying to let you know he needs to go out and you miss his signal and he has an accident by the door, it is your fault and not the dog's. If you missed his signal, then just clean up the mess without making a big deal out of it and try to be more vigilant supervising your dog. You are closer to success than you realize.

If your dog doesn't know how to let you know he needs to go out, please read chapter six for details on teaching him an old trick of ringing a bell when he needs to go out. It will save you a lot of heartache especially if your dog doesn't show any signs of needing to eliminate. This is especially true of the very small breeds. The smaller breeds can be very sneaky, which is why a lot of people think they are harder to train than larger breeds. If you have a smaller breed that resists going outside when it is raining, snowing or very cold, you'll need to pick the dog up and take him to the designated area and wait until he goes. If he doesn't eliminate, bring him back inside and put him in the crate for 30 to 60 minutes and try again.

Sooner or later, your dog will realize that if he doesn't go when he is brought outside, he doesn't get any freedom when he comes back inside. This is probably the number one reason people fail to get their smaller dog housebroken. They will take their dog outside and wait 10, 15, 20 or even 30 minutes for the dog to go to the bathroom. If the dog doesn't do his job, they bring the dog back in and the dog has an accident in the house within minutes. The owner gave the dog freedom in the house before he did his job outside. When the dog fails to eliminate outside, bring the dog back into the house and put him in his crate for 30 to 60 minutes and then try the process again until he does actually go outside. He'll learn that going outside results in freedom and playtime inside. Be consistent and get everyone in your household on the same page so you won't have to clean up accidents.

It may take the smaller dog a little longer to figure out why he is outside and what his job is, but before you know it, your dog will be eliminating almost immediately upon being brought to the designated area. Don't be shy when introducing your dog to the collar and leash. Lead the dog by pulling him to the designated area. If he resists, continue walking (pulling, if necessary) to the spot. If your dog stops and refuses to follow and gets you to stop, he is training you. You could use a rich reward such as a special treat to lure him to the designated area. He may be less likely to resist if you reward him. You want to be careful NOT to use too many treats when trying to get your dog to go straight to the designated spot. Some dogs are distracted or become overly excited with treats and he could possibly forget what he is supposed to be doing when brought to his bathroom spot.

Congratulations! You have completed the most important training your dog will ever need to get him started on the right track. Housebreaking your dog is the first step to building a loving relationship. Socialization and obedience training are the next two steps in the process. To locate a professional trainer near you check out www.dogpro.org to continue your dog's higher education.

I hope to join you on your journey helping you to develop a more loving relationship with your canine companion. Soon I will be releasing several new books. Some of the training topics will include the following:

What Your Dog Trainer Isn't Telling You

How to Stop Jumping and Nipping Forever

Aggression Consultation - When Your Dog Bites

Off Leash in Three Weeks - Training With the E-Collar

Taboo Subject of Discipline

Re-training the Traumatized Dog on the Electric Fence (DVD) Available NOW

I hope that you request my FREE *Training Tips e-newsletter* filled with techniques on any number of training subjects. I have more than 60 articles which have been published over the last 15 years, on my website.

Thank you for purchasing this training book!

Thomas A. Beitz,

Canine Behavior Specialist and Dog Trainer

www.SmartDogSolutions.com

Appendix A
The Basics of Scientific Learning

D r. Pavlov was a Russian physiologist who conducted experiments on dogs in the late 1800's. Pavlov's theory of Classical Conditioning is most often studied in college psychology classes. Pavlov is commonly known for his experiment of ringing a bell and immediately dispensing a small piece of food to a number of dogs. He did this exercise over a period of time and simply observed the dogs' behavior.

As part of the experiment Pavlov rang the bell and withheld the food. Do you remember what the dogs did? They began to salivate. On the surface, an experiment conducted over a hundred years ago doesn't appear to contain much value for the average dog owner today. However, there were two brilliant observations that have contributed significantly to understanding behavior and how dogs learn.

First, he observed that dogs like food. Well, I suppose you didn't need to be a Russian physiologist to figure that out. But secondly and more importantly, it was observed that dogs learn by association. Dogs pair things together that occur simultaneously. From a dog's perspective, if two things occur at the same time, then they are connected to one another.

The dog associated the food with the bell because they occurred at the same time. I'm sure some would say this is an oversimplification, while others have referred to Pavlov's theory of Classical Conditioning as associative learning. In order for a dog to make the association I have described, the two events must be linked in time. They need to occur nearly simultaneously for the dog to pair or link them together.

Subsequent experiments similar to Pavlov's were also conducted by the military around the time of WWII and supported the work of Pavlov. New dog training and behaviorism theories began to emerge at a rate never seen before. As more experiments and testing took place, the use of food in the training process became widely accepted. That is not to say that food wasn't used prior to this time period. But like so many other breakthroughs, once the revelation comes to one person, others seem to embrace it and then take it to the next level. This is one of the reasons why so many animal trainers employ the use of food or treats in the training process today.

It is important to understand training with treats is only one part or aspect of the training process. If you attempt to pitch a training methodology tent around the Classical Conditioning theory alone, inevitably you will find yourself frustrated with the results. Classical Conditioning is a good place to start and the understanding of the connection between timing and association is invaluable. It is important to understand that Classical Conditioning is just one of the two main learning theories embraced by the training community. The other theory commonly associated with training and behaviorism is called Operant Conditioning.

These two learning theories include a number of different aspects of how dogs learn. By emphasizing one aspect of a learning model and neglecting another, you'll end up with dismal results and be very frustrated. I believe that is why so many people struggle training their dog. It isn't that people are not trying, it's that they don't have all the tools. Actually, I believe more people are attempting to train their dog beyond anything I have witnessed in my twenty year dog-training career. The problem is that most people have only a part of what they need to get lasting results. It is like trying to put a puzzle together only to discover that you are missing a couple pieces.

Operant Conditioning was developed by B. F. Skinner in the 1950s. Although Skinner embraced Pavlov's theory of associative learning, he took behavior and learning to a whole new level. I hope you are not thinking that because Skinner's theory was developed over 60 years ago that it is outdated or irrelevant. On the contrary, Skinner's four-part theory of Operant Conditioning continues to be the central learning model used by most dog trainers and behaviorists. However, the secret is that most trainers do not use all four parts of Skinner's theory. They only use two parts, and that is why so many people fail to get the results they desire.

If I were to ask if you've ever heard of positive reinforcement, most people would say "why yes, of course." Positive reinforcement is one part of Skinner's four-part learning model. However, most people would have a difficult time telling me the other three parts because most dog trainers do not teach the rest of the learning model. The theories we learn in school are not necessarily applied in real life learning situations. So as a result, we tend to forget them. It is in these forgotten and often ignored scientific theories that *What Dog Trainers Don't Tell You FREE Report* are revealed.

For a more detailed explanation of Skinner's theory of Operant Conditioning, visit my website. After you have read these easy-to-read articles, you may know more about how dogs learn than the average dog trainer. Find out why some parts of Skinner's theory have been neglected over the past ten to fifteen years and why attempting to train a dog with positive reinforcement alone is like trying to change a light bulb with both hands tied behind your back.

If you want long-lasting results with a high level of reliability, you will need to consider the virtues of other learning models such as Operant Conditioning. Visit my website www.smartdogsolutions.com to read more on this important subject and take your dog to the next level.

Appendix B
Submissive Urinating
&
Excitement Urinating

Submissive urinating is NOT a housebreaking problem. It is a dog's instinctive response to a situation that constitutes a threat to him. Although this problem can be found in older dogs that have been neglected, frightened or inappropriately punished, it generally occurs in younger puppies during their socialization period of development. This behavior can be solved by using a few different techniques but it takes time to build your dog's confidence to overcome the problem.

Before I discuss how to correct the problem, it is necessary to understand why your dog is urinating submissively. Dogs offer many different forms of body language when communicating. A younger, abused, confused or insecure dog may urinate submissively in order to communicate to you, a guest entering your home or another dog that he is perceived as dominant. He wants the person or other dog to know he is submissive and wants to avoid conflict.

You may be offering dominant body language which is contributing to the problem without realizing it. Approaching a dog directly is very confrontational and may cause an insecure dog to feel threatened, so he may urinate to let you know he is not interested in any sort of confrontation or challenge.

Prolonged eye contact with a timid dog can also be very intimidating. Actually, even a brief moment of eye contact can be enough to cause a very submissive dog to urinate. By urinating, your dog is communicating that you are superior to him which is a sign of respect. It can go beyond respect and become fear for the extremely anxious dog. That is why disciplining your dog for submissive urinating is completely counterproductive. In fact, it will make the problem worse. If your dog is urinating because it is being submissive and you discipline the dog, he will more than likely feel he is not being submissive enough and then resort to emptying his bladder rather than just a piddle in an attempt to convince you that he respects your authority.

There are two things which you DO NOT want to do if your puppy or dog is urinating submissively. First, you do not want to discipline or correct the dog. I know I just repeated what I said in the previous paragraph, however after working with thousands of frustrated dog owners over the past 20 years, I know some things need to be repeated. Secondly, you do not want to console your dog to make him feel better about what he has just done. Both of these responses from you will make the problem worse. It is a normal human response to console someone that is afraid or insecure. Unfortunately, your dog is not a human and attempting to console your dog for any inappropriate behavior will result in reinforcing the behavior.

How to Correct the Problem of Submissive Urinating

There are several ways to help solve this annoying problem and they both require patience and time. One of the first things you can do to solve the problem is to begin to be aware of your body language when approaching your dog. Begin by approaching your dog on an angle or from the side rather than head on which can be perceived as confrontational and dominant. When speaking with your dog use a softer voice to communicate your requests. This will help to build confidence in your dog. Loud, deep voices may intimidate your dog so try to avoid yelling at your dog even if he has had an accident. Your body language and the tone of voice will help to build your dog's confidence.

Approaching a Timid Dog

When you first enter a room your dog is in, ignore the dog for about two to five minutes. Even if your dog is in a crate, do not say anything to him. Gradually move over to the crate and casually open the crate door and calmly walk to the door you typically use to take your dog outside to do his business. Some dogs are so anxious that even after five minutes they still may feel the need to piddle when you try to attach the leash to your dog's collar. You may find it helpful to make the leash into a noose and slip it over your dog's head and take the dog outside rather than trying to clip the leash onto the collar. It is faster, and you can do it without touching your dog. Continue to be as unemotional and quiet as possible. If your dog does happen to piddle in the process, remember that modifying this behavior takes patience and time. Ignore the accident and follow the procedure. The next time you approach your dog, try to be more cautious than you were the previous time.

This exercise applies to your family as well as your guests. Although they may not be taking your puppy outside to eliminate, they need to remain quiet and calm. Sudden movements, loud noises and dominant body language may all constitute a threat resulting in your dog piddling. You can expect accidents along the way in the process. When accidents happen, take your dog outside, give him a chance to eliminate taking pressure off his bladder and clean up the mess after you come back inside. It is a good idea to take your puppy outside before company comes to the house, giving him an opportunity to eliminate which will help to mitigate the problem. If the problem is more severe, have your company greet your dog outside. Let the dog approach your company on his terms after he feels comfortable with the person visiting. Don't let your all-knowing, well meaning friend force himself on your puppy. By allowing strangers to push your puppy into socializing with them, it may actually make the problem worse. They may have good intentions, but good intentions don't train dogs.

Obedience Training

Another way of building your dog's confidence is to begin doing some obedience exercises. By teaching your dog the basic commands such as heel, sit and stay, coming when called and the down command, you will be establishing a more exact means of communicating with your dog. If he genuinely knows what sit and stay means, he will be conditioned to focus on your command rather than the object of his insecurity.

Although I am a big believer in consequence based obedience training which includes discipline and correction, the time to discipline your dog is not during the training phase when attempting to overcome submissive urinating. In fact, you should focus on rewarding your dog for complying with a command during the training. It is harder for your dog to urinate submissively if he is eating a treat. If he is thinking about a treat he can't be thinking about urinating at the same time. The treat becomes a distraction for your dog directing his attention away from whatever is triggering the submissive behavior. The treat should be very small, something that can be consumed in about two seconds. Your puppy doesn't need to be rewarded with a sixteen ounce milk bone just for sitting.

With that being said, it is important to make the distinction as to when the treat should be given and when it should be withheld. We want the dog to understand he is being given a treat for simply complying with the request to sit or whatever command you have given him. Just be careful that you are not rewarding the dog for piddling either by giving him a treat or petting and praising him. The treat is only given for a reward when your dog obeys your command without piddling.

Obedience training is also a great way to observe your own body language to see what things you may be doing that are triggering this behavior. It is a good idea to do these exercises outside. If your dog piddles outside, you don't need to clean it up and you can see what you may have done that caused your dog to piddle so that you can avoid that in your next training exercise. As your dog learns some of the basic commands such as sit and stay, heel and coming when called, it is a good idea to gradually begin to introduce him to new people and situations. Over time his confidence will increase and you'll have overcome this temporary behavior problem.

Excitement Urinating

Excitement urinating is generally found in high energy excitable puppies and dogs which have not fully developed bladder control. It is important to understand that just as submissive urinating is not a housebreaking problem, neither is excitement urinating. Most excitable puppies do not even realize they are piddling. All of the exercises that apply to submissive urinating apply to excitement urinating especially when it comes to obedience training. Obedience training will help you to develop restraint in your dog which will help to calm him down in different situations.

High energy dogs need structure to help them focus on the task at hand. This can only be accomplished when obedience training is done on a leash so you can control your dog. As you gain control of your dog, he will naturally learn restraint. If you permit your dog to run around when company comes to visit or whatever event may trigger this excitable behavior, the dog will grow into the urinating behavior, not out of it. You need to restrain the dog when people come to visit especially when you are inside your house. Teaching your dog to heel or doing a sit-stay or a down-stay will be the best obedience exercise you could teach the excitable dog.

Some dogs are so excitable that you could walk out of a room for five minutes and upon returning the dog is just as excitable as when you first entered the room. This problem can be corrected by using the following exercise. Leave a six foot leash on your dog to drag around one room in your house because you want to limit how much freedom you give your dog. When you enter the room, grab the leash and begin an obedience exercise for about five minutes. Then leave the room for several minutes. Upon returning to the room, grab the leash and give the dog the same obedience exercise as before. Repeat this exercise three or four times per day. Try having other family members do this exercise with your dog also so he doesn't associate all of his training with just you. Something very interesting will begin to happen.

Each time you or someone else enters the room, your dog will begin to recognize that it means work. After a period of time you will begin to recognize your dog becoming less excited when you enter the room. When you begin to see your dog just relaxing and chilling out, at that point you can begin to cut back on the exercises. He'll learn that if he remains calm he can avoid working, he'll begin to calm down on his own. Being calm is rewarded by not having to work in an obedience exercise. Continue to let your dog drag the leash around so that if you need to intervene, you will have the leash to grab to get him to settle down.

After you observe your dog settling down you can begin to initiate some playtime. Playtime should be initiated by you and not your dog. After you have played with your dog for five or ten minutes, then grab the leash and stop the play and move into an obedience exercise. By interrupting the play time with obedience training you will build a higher level of restraint in your dog. As your dog matures physiologically and his bladder develops stronger muscles, the excitement urinating will stop. It will not happen overnight and you may see him regress during the training phase, but stick with it and before you know it not only will you have solved the excitable urinating problem, you'll have an obedient, well-trained dog.

If you do not have your dog on some training program that is working for you, please check out my website for my book, "Off Leash in Three Weeks" which teaches you how to train your excitable dog to obey you off leash anywhere you go in just three weeks. Training your dog off leash is one of the best ways to give your dog exercise which will help to calm him down. The book will be available in the spring of 2013.

Visit my website www.SmartDogSolutions.com and request my FREE REPORT, What Your Dog Trainer Isn't Telling You. My FREE REPORT reveals many of the secrets professional dog trainers don't want you to know regarding the easy to understand science behind dog training. Over the past 10 to 15 years dog training techniques and technology have significantly improved and what used to take months to train a dog can now be accomplished in literally three weeks with only 15 minutes of effort per day, saving you time and money.

Summary

If you discipline your puppy for urinating, you will be making him feel more insecure. That generally results in more submissive urinating. By consoling him for urinating, you will be rewarding him for urinating. He may actually begin to think that you want him to urinate when you or someone else approaches him. Telling him, it's alright, it's ok, or petting him will communicate to him that it is actually alright, when it is not.

Watch your body language. Be careful to approach your dog in a non-confrontational way. Limit your eye contact and give your dog several minutes to get used to you or visitors before making physical contact with him.

As you begin obedience training exercises with your dog, you will be building your dog's confidence as well as his attention level.

About the Author

Tom Beitz confronts each day with one question: "How can I help more people solve their pet's problems?" Breaking into the dog training industry in 1995, Tom attended the Puppy and Dog Training Academy (PDTA) where he was certified to work with house pets, solving difficult behavior problems and obedience training. He was one of the first dog trainers in Western New York who offered private lessons in the home as an option to the sometimes awkward group class.

Tom participated in the Canine Behavior Study offered through Cornell University conducted by Dr. Dorothy Houpt specializing in the remediation of extremely difficult behavior problems. He was certified through the Triple Crown Training Academy in Hutto, Texas for a special certification known as Gentle Touch Training (GTT). GTT is a cutting edge method of training which uses a pet-friendly approach to training a dog on the electric fence. He also received a certification from Sit Means Sit, No Limitation E-collar training program.

Tom lives in South Dayton, New York with his wife, Tricia, and his stepson, Adam, on a 25 acre hobby farm. He offers a variety of training programs ranging from group classes to private lessons in the home to boarding school programs. He has had over 80 dog training articles published in various newspapers throughout Western New York.

Tom has worked with the Humane Society and many public schools and day care facilities offering FREE seminars on important dog-related subjects including Bite Prevention, Dog Safety and Preventing Bad Behavior. He is a charter member of the International Association of Canine Professionals (IACP) with numerous articles published in their trade journal SafeHands.

If you or your group would be interested in scheduling a workshop, training clinic or a phone consultation, please feel free to contact me to make arrangements.

Thomas A. Beitz, Canine Behavior Specialist

Smart Dog Solutions

P.O. Box 274

Hamburg, New York 14075

Email - Tom@SmartDogSolutions.com

Phone - 716-628-0651

Website - www.SmartDogSolutions.com

CPSIA information can be obtained at www.ICGtesting.com
Printed in the USA
BVOW03s1041220114

342660BV00010B/446/P